What does the Bible really say about...

ADAM & EVE

Thomas Fretwell

"To my wife Sarah, thank you for everything" - Proverbs 31:10

Adam and Eve
Thomas Fretwell

ISBN 978-1-84625-631-8

Copyright © Day One Publications 2019

Cover design and typesetting by Dave Hewer Design (davehewer.com)
Printed by Orchard Press Cheltenham Ltd

British Library Cataloguing in Publication Data available.

No part of this publication may be reproduced, or stored in a retrieval system, or transmitted, in any form or by any means, mechanical, electronic, photocopying, recording or otherwise, without the prior permission of Day One Publications.

Scripture quotations are from The Holy Bible, English Standard Version® (ESV®), copyright © 2001 by Crossway, a publishing ministry of Good News Publishers. Used by permission. All rights reserved.

Contents

1. Why all the fuss? 1
2. Fact or fiction 7
3. The creation of Adam 13
4. The creation of Eve 19
5. The fall of Adam and Eve 25
6. Jesus, Adam and Eve 37
7. Paul, Adam and Eve 45
8. The last Adam 51

Why all the fuss?

Where do we come from? What does it mean to be human? These questions are fundamental to life. If we ever want to truly grasp who we are as human beings, we need to understand where we came from. Traditionally, the Christian answer has been that mankind is the progeny of Adam and Eve, the first two humans created by God. As such, mankind is separate from the animal kingdom, endowed with inherent worth and dignity, the only creature given the privilege of being made in the image of God (Genesis 1:26-27). Christian theology has historically understood the pivotal role of Adam and Eve in the grand narrative of redemption. Their story is integral to many of

> "If we ever want to truly grasp who we are as human beings, we need to understand where we came from."

the central doctrines of Christianity, especially the doctrines of sin and salvation.

The greatest challenge to this understanding of humanity has come from the theory of evolution. The evolutionary view of mankind, that humans evolved from an ape-like ancestor, proposed by Charles Darwin in the nineteenth century, radically transformed the prevailing view of mankind's origins, shifting it away from the biblical understanding of Adam and Eve to the evolutionary view of Darwin. Noticing that this shift created a sharp contrast between these two widely differing accounts of human origins, many in the Church tried to invent ways to accommodate the evolutionary story into the Bible. This inevitably resulted in having to change the way the Bible is understood and interpreted. The greatest tragedy in this new reading of the Bible is

> *"Our understanding of Adam and Eve is pivotal to understanding the Gospel. Sin came into the word through Adam, and Jesus came to save us from our sins."*

that the historical Adam and Eve have either been demoted to the level of symbolic metaphors, or they are the descendants of lower primates. Such alterations completely undermine the authority of the Bible itself.

This departure from the straight forward meaning of the text creates more problems than it solves. Once the authority of the Word of God is undermined, the teaching of Scripture unravels. Our understanding of Adam and Eve is pivotal to understanding the Gospel. Sin came into the word through Adam, and Jesus came to save us from our sins (Romans 5:12-21; 1 Corinthians 15:22-55). The connection is so clear that even many atheists have realised that if they can do away with Adam and Eve, they can do away with Christianity itself. Listen to the words of Frank Zindler, head of the American Atheists:

> *The most devastating thing though that biology did to Christianity was the discovery of biological evolution. Now that we know that Adam and Eve never were real people the central myth of*

> *Christianity is destroyed. **If there never was an Adam and Eve**, there never was an original sin … if there never was an original sin, there is no need for salvation. If there is no need for salvation, there is no need for a saviour. And I submit that puts Jesus into the ranks of the unemployed. I think that evolution is absolutely the death knell of Christianity.*
>
> Frank Zindler, debate with William L. Craig (video) Zondervan, 1996.

In view of such challenging words, it is vital to understand that the Bible portrays Adam and Eve as real historical people; they were the first two humans ever created and with them the biblical panorama of sin and redemption begins.

Fact or fiction

The number of evangelicals who reject the historicity of Adam and Eve is steadily increasing. Many will claim that the story of Adam and Eve is not meant to be taken literally. Instead, it is a symbolic story to teach us theological and moral truths about the nature of man. Still others, who have accepted the evolutionary view of humanity, will say that Adam and Eve did exist, but not exactly as the Bible portrays. Rather, they have evolved from a lineage of ape-like creatures, and they became "human" only when God breathed a soul into them. Such views find absolutely no support in the Scriptures and have been artificially imposed onto the text to

> "The Bible leaves absolutely no room for the view that Adam and Eve were anything other than real historical people."

support ideas from outside the Bible.

The Bible leaves absolutely no room for the view that Adam and Eve were anything other than real historical people. The testimony is clear from both the Old and New Testaments, although, as many people point out, Adam and Eve feature heavily in the early narrative of Genesis, they seemingly play a less prominent role in the rest of the Old Testament. However, this does not negate the fact that their presence in the early chapters of Genesis provides an explanatory foundation for much of what follows in the biblical story.

The book of Genesis is written as one unified historical narrative. The history of the early chapters (1-11) cannot be divorced from that of the later chapters (12-50), which are rarely contested by scholars. The repeated occurrence of the Hebrew expression '*toledoth*', "these are the generations of", or "this is the written account of" (*Genesis 5:1*) ensure that no schism can be placed into the narrative as the literary structure is consistent throughout the book. In addition, the detailed genealogies in Genesis 5 and 11, which connect Adam with more prominent biblical characters such as Noah and Abraham, provide clear historical evidence that Moses, as the author of Genesis, considered Adam to be the literal historical ancestor of humanity.

> *"To claim that undisputed historical characters... somehow descended from "symbolic" persons is theologically flawed and historically pointless..."*

Outside of Genesis there is still a wealth of evidence which proves that the Scriptures teach Adam was a historical person. The consistent use of genealogies is perhaps the most striking argument for historicity. The whole purpose of a genealogy is to trace a person's historical lineage. If a genealogy was populated with mythical or symbolic figures, the whole thing would become meaningless. To claim that undisputed historical characters like Abraham or King David, somehow descended from "symbolic" persons is theologically flawed and historically pointless as well as highly illogical.

This poses a problem for those who believe that

Adam was not a literal historical person. The genealogy in 1 Chronicles 1–9 traces the ancestry of the sons of Israel all the way back to Adam. There is no hint in this nine-chapter list of names that we are to interpret them in any other way than real historical people. Equally as problematic for those denying a literal Adam is the genealogy in Luke 3:23-38, which traces the lineage of the Messiah. First, the fact that a New Testament author like Luke, whose historical accuracy is well documented, utilises these Old Testament genealogies to show the lineage of Jesus, points to their accuracy and historicity. Second, if the messianic line originates with a mythical figure, who is only included to teach theological truths, then it totally undermines the theological argument of Luke who is demonstrating that the Messiah is a Jew from the tribe of David. Luke's second New Testament volume, the book of Acts, also implicitly confirms the early belief

> "The reference to 'one man' clearly teaches that all humanity can trace their existence back to Adam, just as the genealogies show."

that Adam was the literal and historical ancestor of the human race. In Paul's famous sermon on Mars hill, where he preaches the gospel to the Athenian philosophers and idol worshippers, he states that God, "made from *one man* every nation of mankind to live on all the face of the earth" (Acts 17:26). The reference to "one man" clearly teaches that all humanity can trace their existence back to Adam, just as the genealogies show.

The creation of Adam

The Bible is very clear: humans and animals have two separate lineages. In no way do these two lines cross at any point. We learn from Genesis 1:27 that Adam was created in the "image of God". This is important as it affords humanity a uniqueness that is not given to anything else in the created order. Humans are made to resemble God in certain ways. This image is not a physical likeness, because God is spirit (John 4:24), but it does imply there is a spiritual component to man, referred to as the soul (Genesis 2:7; Luke 10:27). Mankind's cognitive faculties are also far superior to the animal world, providing a sharp distinction between man and beast. Mankind has the ability for advanced reasoning, superior emotional capabilities and the freedom of choice. Men and women are also endowed with minds that are capable of communing

> "Mankind has been given an inherent moral awareness, the ability to choose between good and evil, right and wrong."

with God through prayer and expressing themselves in worship. Another aspect to this "image" is that people are created as moral beings. Mankind has been given an inherent moral awareness, the ability to choose between good and evil, right and wrong. The Bible refers to this as a conscience (Romans 2:14-15) and it means that people are morally responsible agents. These factors determine that mankind is created to be utterly unique.

In Genesis chapter 2, which serves largely as a recapitulation of Genesis 1:1-2:3, except that it concentrates more on the creation of Adam, we learn that God created Adam from the dust of the earth (Genesis 2:7). The text is very clear that Adam was alone at this point. It says, "there was no man to cultivate the ground" (Genesis 2:5). This excludes all explanatory models that teach Adam was selected from an already existing group of humans, either as an archetype of humanity or a tribal chief. The text of Genesis says that God "formed" (2:7) Adam from the "dust of the ground". The Hebrew verb used to describe this creative act is *yatsar,* which means to 'mould', 'sculpt', or to 'form'. It is a word that describes the activity of a potter (Jeremiah 18:2) emphasizing the personal involvement of the potter in the creative process. The use of this word in Genesis 2:7 shows that God was personally involved in the creation of Adam.

God formed Adam from the "dust of the ground" (Genesis 2:7), this is clearly saying that Adam was formed from material previously created by God. This is clear by the later declaration of judgement in Genesis 3:19 where God says to Adam, "till you return to the ground, for out of it you were taken; for you are dust, and to dust you shall return".

The important point to note from the context of Genesis 2:7 is that there is no intermediary process involved in the creation of Adam. Therefore, to

> "...there is no intermediary process involved in the creation of Adam."

insert the millions of years of evolutionary time needed to change lower, pre-existing hominids into humans, is exegetically untenable. In this verse there is no gap in time and no indication that Adam evolved from pre-existing life forms; rather, the direct and most straight forward reading is that Adam was formed from the ground and only became a living creature when God "breathed into his nostrils the breath of life".

> "The formation process from material elements alone did not create life."

A living soul

After God breathed into Adam the breath of life he became a living creature (Genesis 2:7). This is the biblical record of how the first living human came into existence. The formation process from material elements alone did not create life. Rather, it required a direct act of God to bring Adam to life. This composition is another distinguishing factor belonging to mankind. Adam consisted of both physical and non-physical parts. We see both mentioned in the text of Genesis. The physical body, made from the "dust of the Ground", and the non-physical soul, from the "breath of life".

The creation of Eve

The creation account of Eve is equally unique. In contrast to Adam, who God formed from non-living matter, Eve is said to be created from: Adam himself. In Genesis chapter 2 we are given more details about the events of day six of creation. We encounter the first instance where God describes something as "not good". It is the fact that Adam is alone (Genesis 2:18). During the process of giving names to the animals Adam would have been acutely aware that "there was not found a helper fit for him" (Genesis 2:20). God's solution is to create "a helper fit for him". Only another being created equally in the image of God would be suitable for Adam. The term "helper", does not indicate a difference in nature, only

> "Only another being created equally in the image of God would be suitable for Adam."

in function. She was to be his spiritual counterpart, she would complete mankind, being his perfect companion in every way. The two sexes would complement each other in a perfect union.

The first surgery

In Genesis 2:21-25 it says that God put Adam into a deep sleep and took one of his ribs in order to make the woman. While Adam slept God removed his rib and then healed up the wound in Adam's side. From this rib the text says that God made a woman. The Hebrew word used here is different from the word "formed" (*yatsar*) used in the creation account of Adam. The verb used for Eve's formation is *banah* and it means to "build" or "construct". It is more applicable to something made from flesh rather than the ground. God constructed the woman as his final act of creation.

> "The fact that Adam and Eve share the same physical material is clear from Adam's exclamation..."

One flesh

The creation narrative's account of Eve, in which she is made from Adams rib, is significant in many ways. First, the fact that Eve was created in such a way precludes any evolutionary claim that Eve arose from a pre-existing hominid line that was separate from Adam's. Second, it was vital that Eve be a descendant of Adam because it was the descendants of Adam that Jesus came to save. Jesus has to be related by blood to those he redeems. He achieved this by becoming part of the lineage of Adam through the incarnation (Philippians 2:5-11; Luke 3:23-38). The fact that Adam and Eve share the same physical material is clear from Adam's exclamation when he first saw her: "this at last is bone of my bones and flesh of my flesh, she shall be called woman, for she was taken out of man" (Genesis 2:23). The fact that all people are descended from the union of Adam and Eve is reflected in the name Eve, which means "mother of all living" (Genesis 3:20).

The first marriage

In the secular evolutionary worldview, marriage appeared as a development within the cultural evolution of human societies; it is a social convention and nothing more. The Bible teaches that marriage is a divine institution, given as a gift to mankind by God, and it is based upon the complementary nature of the two sexes. God created Adam and Eve and ordained the institution of marriage in the book of Genesis. This event supplies the precedent for all marriages that follow. Marriage is defined by God to be between one man and one woman for life. Genesis 2:24 says:

> *Therefore a man shall leave his father and his mother and hold fast to his wife, and they shall become one flesh.*

Marriage involves the sexual and spiritual union of a man and a woman when they become "one flesh". This means that all forms of sexual intimacy are to be enjoyed only within the marriage relationship. Any form of sexual relationship outside of marriage is contrary to God's intended design (Exodus 20:14; Hebrews 13:4).

The fall of Adam and Eve

The "Fall" is the term used to refer to the first sin committed by Adam and Eve in the Garden of Eden. Up until this point, they lived harmoniously with each other and exercised dominion over nature. They enjoyed the blessing of unbroken fellowship with their Creator in the Garden (Genesis 3:8). There was no death, pain, suffering or sickness in the world at this point. God placed the newly created man, Adam, in the Garden to "work it and keep it" (Genesis 2:15). God gave him permission to eat from "every tree of the garden" (Genesis 2:16). There was only one exception: the tree of the knowledge of good and evil. God prohibited him from eating the fruit of this tree and issued this warning to Adam should

> "Adam and Eve... lived harmoniously with each other and exercised dominion over nature."

he disobey: "for in the day that you eat of it you shall surely die" (Genesis 2:17).

The serpent's temptations

At this point in the narrative we are introduced to another character, the serpent. Satan, through the guise of a serpent, communicates with the woman, Eve, attempting to get her to disobey God. The serpent is described as being more "crafty" than the other beasts (Genesis 3:1). Satan's deceptive strategy is to first get Eve to doubt the word of God: "Did God actually say, 'You shall not eat of any tree in the garden'?", the serpent asks (Genesis 3:1). It was a subtle twisting of the original command which only prohibited eating from one particular tree, surely meant to give the impression that the command from God was overly burdensome and unreasonable. Eve responds

> "Satan is making God out to be selfish, purposefully withholding something that could be good for them."

to the serpent saying that God had actually said, "You shall not eat of the fruit of the tree that is in the midst of the garden, neither shall you touch it, lest you die" (Genesis 3:3). She is correct except for her addition of the phrase "do not touch" which was absent from the original command.

The first lie

Satan now moves from trying to induce doubt in God's word to outright denial of God's command. Satan responds to Eve; "You will not surely die?" (Genesis 3:4). This defiant statement contradicts the direct warning from God and implicitly undermines his character by suggesting that He lacks the ability to fulfil His own commands. Satan further denigrates God's character by accusing Him of giving them this command to make sure that they do not acquire the same knowledge that He has; "For God knows that when you eat of it your eyes will be opened, and you will be like God, knowing good and evil" (Genesis 3:5). In effect Satan is making God out to be selfish, purposefully withholding something that could be good for them. Satan has now put his word in opposition to God's. To deny God's word is to side with Satan and choose evil. Satan is the one who lies; Jesus calls him "the father of lies" (John 8:44).

Eve is deceived

In Genesis 3:6 we read that Eve ultimately succumbed to the lies of Satan and ate the fruit from the tree of the knowledge of good and evil. She saw that "the tree was good for food, and that it was a delight to the eyes, and that the tree was desirable to make *one* wise" (Genesis 3:6). The fact that Eve ate the fruit with the expectation that it would "make one wise" is a clear indication that she had been deceived by Satan's lie and, in fact, did think that somehow God was withholding the key to true knowledge from them. In this scene we also see her elevating her own desires above the Word of God. Personal exaltation along with satanic deception will always result in a rejection of God's command. The act that sealed her fate is stated simply, "she took from its fruit and ate".

> "Eve is said to have been deceived whereas Adam is held responsible for the Fall..."

Adam sins

The Bible frequently differentiates between Eve's act of eating the fruit and what Adam did. Eve is said to have been deceived (2 Corinthians 11:3; 1 Timothy 2:13-14) whereas Adam is held responsible for the Fall; the blame for the entrance of sin into the world is laid upon him (Romans 5:12). Adam's disobedience in eating the fruit was an act of wilful defiance towards God and a clear rejection of his command. The text does not provide the reasons for Adam's sin, it simply records that Eve, "gave also to her husband with her, and he ate" (Genesis 3:6). The text implies that Adam was with Eve during this time, he may have even witnessed the conversation between the serpent and Eve, yet failed to exercise his leadership role and intervene, "Adam was not deceived..." (1 Timothy 2:14), as the federal head of the human race he was guilty. The consequences were immediate and tragic.

Eyes were opened

The text records that, after eating the forbidden fruit, "the eyes of both of them were opened, and they knew that they were naked" (Genesis 3:6). The serpent was correct: their eyes were opened. But the results were not what Satan had promised. Instead, they had now become personally acquainted with moral evil and would personally experience its tragic consequences. They now experienced a sense of shame and guilt. In a futile attempt to cover their nakedness they "sewed fig leaves together and made themselves loin coverings" (Genesis 3:7). This act stands out as the first attempt at man-made religion – a way of

> "The most tragic result of sin is the separation it causes between man and God."

trying to cover our own sin (Isaiah 64:6).

Broken fellowship

The most tragic result of sin is the separation it causes between man and God (Isaiah 59:2). Previously, Adam and Eve had enjoyed unbroken fellowship with God as He walked in the garden with them (Genesis 3:8). Now, for the first time, Adam and Eve felt fear in the presence of God and "hid themselves from the presence of the Lord God among the trees of the garden" (Genesis 3:8). The perfect union they had previously enjoyed with the Creator was gone; they had died spiritually, and from this moment the process of physical death began too. The presence of God now inspired a sense of fear and shame. Man was now a fallen creature.

A chance to confess

When God came to the garden to see Adam and Eve he offered them an opportunity to confess what they have done by asking two rhetorical questions, "Where are you?" (Genesis 3:9) and, "Who told you that you were naked?" (Genesis 3:11). Obviously, God, being omniscient, knew full well the answers to these questions, but he still gave them the chance to confess before him. Unfortunately, with unrepentant hearts Adam and Eve begin trying to shift the blame. Adam first blamed God, "the woman you gave me…", then he blamed Eve, "she gave me from the tree…". When God asked Eve what she has done, she responded by blaming the serpent, "the serpent deceived me" (Genesis 3:13). Having established guilt God now pronounced judgement.

Threefold judgement

God proceeds to issue judgement, first upon the serpent, then the creation as a whole and then Adam and Eve. The serpent is to be cursed above all cattle and every beast of the field. It will crawl on its belly and eat the dust of the ground. There will be enmity between the serpent and mankind. Finally, the serpent will injure the seed of the women but will receive a mortal wound in return (Genesis 3:14-15). This "future" seed is often interpreted to be the first reference to the Messiah. In the Bible family lines are usually traced through the male line but now this seed is said to come in a unique way through the seed of the woman. We learn later from the Scriptures that the Messiah would come without a human father through the virginal conception (Isaiah 7:14; Matthew 1:18). God next pronounces judgment upon the woman: she will experience increased pain during childbirth and there will be hierarchal confusion within the marital relationship, and a battle for supremacy between the sexes in general (Genesis 3:16). Finally, God judges the man. Adam failed to exercise proper headship when he ate the fruit. He was given dominion over the creation and

> "In the Bible family lines are usually traced through the male line but now this seed is said to come in a unique way through the seed of the woman."

his rebellion would alter this relationship. The ground was now cursed by God, thorns and thistles will mark creation, and it will take extreme effort to produce food from the earth (Genesis 3:17-18). This indicates that the whole of creation would suffer the consequences of the fall (Romans 8:18-25). God then tells Adam that he will suffer the penalties for disobedience that he was warned about in Genesis 2:17, the most serious of which is, "you shall surely die". God also tells Adam that he will toil until "he returns to the ground, because from it you were taken; For you are dust, and to dust you shall return" (Genesis 3:19). It is an unmistakable reference to the physical death that would now encompass the whole of creation.

Clothed and expelled

The final act of God before he removes them from the paradise of Eden is to make "garments of skin for Adam and his wife" (Genesis 3:21). Adam and Eve had covered themselves with fig leaves and now God would have to kill one or more animals and use skins to cover the sinful pair. In this we see a hint of the greater redemption that is being foreshadowed by animal sacrifices, ultimately pointing to the once and for all sacrifice of the Messiah. As Adam and Eve watched an innocent animal being sacrificed to cover the shame of their sin, it served as an object lesson that, "without the shedding of blood there is no forgiveness of sins" (Hebrews 9:22).

Jesus, Adam and Eve

There is ample evidence from the New Testament that Jesus believed the book of Genesis to be historically true. On many occasions he references events from the early chapters of Genesis, such as the flood of Noah (Matthew 24:37-39) and the destruction of Sodom and Gomorrah (Luke 17:28-32). As Christians, Jesus is the highest authority we have, so it is extremely important to make sure our views align with his. Jesus had a very high view of Scripture and believed it to be the Word of God (Mark 7:8-13). He clearly believed that all Scripture was inspired, right down to the very words and letters (Matthew 5:17-18). He knew that it was truth (John 17:17) and that Scripture could not be broken (John 10:35). Considering this, we should take what Jesus said about Adam and

> "As Christians, Jesus is the highest authority we have..."

Eve to be the final word, especially as we are all exhorted to have "the mind of Christ" (1 Corinthians 2:16).

Settling a dispute

One key text is Matthew 19:4-6, where Jesus is involved in a dispute with the Pharisees over the legality of divorce. To authoritatively settle the argument, Jesus first quotes from Genesis 1:27:

> *He answered, "Have you not read that he who created them from the beginning made them male and female?*

Jesus builds his theological case concerning divorce upon the creation account and the first marriage of Adam and Eve. The implication is that this is clearly a real historical event involving real people who had a real marriage. If Adam and Eve were not real people, then the argument completely loses its force. Furthermore, Jesus continues his response by citing Genesis 2:24,

"Therefore a man shall leave his father and his mother and hold fast to his wife, and the two shall become one flesh'?" He then adds, "So they are no longer two but one flesh. What therefore God has joined together, let not man separate" (Matthew 19:6). His theological conclusion about the two becoming one is predicated upon the historical account of Adam and Eve becoming one in Genesis. To claim that Adam and Eve were anything but real historical people and that the account in Genesis is mythological is to completely undercut the argument given by Jesus. Worse, it implies that his understanding is mistaken, clearly an unacceptable conclusion.

> "To claim that Adam and Eve were anything but real historical people... is to completely undercut the argument given by Jesus."

No room for deep time

Another important element is brought out in a parallel account of this same text. In the response recorded in

Mark's Gospel Jesus says:

> *"But from the **beginning of creation**, "God made them male and female."* Mark 10:6

Jesus quotes Genesis 1:27 in referencing the creation of Adam and Eve and specifies that this event occurred at the "beginning of Creation". Jesus places humans at the beginning of earth history, on day six of creation

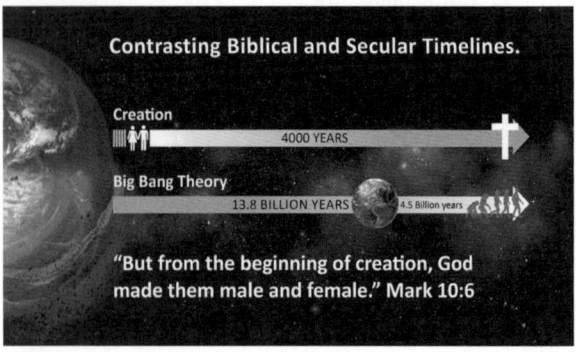

week, not millions of years afterwards. In the prevailing secular evolutionary view, the universe is over 13.8

billion years old, the earth being around 4.5 billion years old and modern humans are only said to have existed in the last one hundred thousand years of that time. This places humans at the end of the creation timeline, not the beginning, and this contradicts what Jesus clearly believed and taught.

The verse clearly shows that Jesus accepted the biblical timescale of earth's origin and the supernatural creation of Adam and Eve at the beginning of creation. The verse makes no sense if billions of years of deep time must be inserted into the timeline, along with millions of years of evolutionary change responsible for turning early hominids into *Homo sapiens*.

The blood of Abel

Another indicator that Jesus understood the Genesis account in a straight forward manner and believed Adam and Eve to be real people is found in Luke's Gospel. This passage is yet another encounter with the Pharisees. Jesus rebukes the Pharisees, saying,

"Therefore also the Wisdom of God said, 'I will send them prophets and apostles, some of whom they will kill and persecute,' so that the blood of all the prophets, shed from the foundation of the world, may be charged against this generation, from the blood of Abel to the blood of Zechariah, who perished between the altar and the sanctuary" (Luke 11:49-51).

Two observations from this text are relevant. Firstly, Jesus states that "the blood of the prophets" had been shed "from the foundation of the earth", obviously implying that prophets, i.e. humans, have been around since the beginning.

> "Jesus clearly believed in the supernatural creation of Adam and Eve..."

This reference is only understandable if we take the beginning to be day six of creation week. It does not make sense to speak of "the foundation of the world" if humans really did not exist until the *very* end of over 4.5 billion years of earth's history; when 99.99% of it had passed. Secondly, Jesus references both Abel and Zechariah together, as real historical characters. This is clear because he even specifies the location of Zechariah's death (2 Chronicles 24:21). What is significant about this is that Abel was the son of Adam and Eve (Genesis 4:2). In order to believe that Abel was historical it must mean categorically that his parents were also historical. Jesus clearly believed in the supernatural creation of Adam and Eve, the first two humans as recorded in the book of Genesis. To try and imply anything different is to contort the text beyond all reasonable meaning.

Paul, Adam and Eve

The apostle Paul is considered to be the premier theologian of the New Testament and is responsible for writing thirteen of the twenty-seven books of the New Testament. There are many cases where Paul constructs his theological arguments upon the historicity of Adam and Eve. Such instances prove that the narratives found in the creation account of Genesis are taken as authoritative by the biblical authors and, therefore, should continue to be for us today.

Paul and justification

One such text that is found in Paul's major theological treatise, the book of Romans. Here Paul uses Adam to create a contrast with Jesus. In Romans 5:12 Paul argues that, "just as sin came into the world through one man, and death through sin, and so death spread to all men because all sinned". The reference to "one man" clearly points back to the first sin of Adam in the garden of Eden. Paul argues that through this sin, death entered the world and spread to all of humanity. He says that "death reigned from Adam to Moses" (Romans 5:14). Pivotally for Paul, sin is connected to Adam, which now becomes the historical foundation for the solution to sin offered in Christ. Paul writes that, "For if many died through one man's trespass, much more have the grace of God and the free gift by the grace of that one-man Jesus Christ abounded for many" (Romans 5:15). The "trespass" is again a reference to Adam's sin. He even references the ensuing judgment that God issued afterwards, "the judgment following one trespass brought condemnation, but the free gift following many trespasses brought justification" (Romans 5:16). In this extended passage

> "...if Paul is basing his argument for justification on the reality of Adam's sin... then it must be integral to the entire gospel."

Paul is arguing that because of the disobedience of Adam, "death reigned through that one man", and that this "one trespass led to condemnation for all

> "The foundation of the requirement for Christ's work of Justification is the Fall of mankind through Adam."

men". However, his point is made in the contrast that "one act of righteousness leads to justification and life for all men", and that, "by the one man's obedience the many will be made righteous". This is referring to Jesus Christ, who was "obedient to the point of death, even death on a cross" (Philippians 2:8).

Here is what we must understand: if Paul is basing his argument for justification on the reality of Adam's sin in Genesis, then it must be integral to the entire gospel. Surely logic entails that if Adam is not, in fact, a real person, then there is no need for a real person to die for his mythical sin? If Adam was not historical, Paul's argument would collapse. The foundation of the requirement for Christ's work of Justification is the Fall of mankind through Adam.

Paul and Eve

Paul also refers to Eve on two occasions in his writings and by doing so, he explicitly confirms the historicity of the Genesis narrative. In 1 Timothy 2:13 Paul is teaching about the differences in functional roles between men and women in the Church. In this argument he quotes the Genesis account:

> *For Adam was formed first, then Eve;*
> 1 Timothy 2:13

This is a very clear statement by Paul, indicating that he believed Genesis 2 to be historical. He not only affirmed the correct order of creation given in Genesis, a fact he also confirms elsewhere (1 Corinthians 11:8), but he goes further to state:

> *Adam was not deceived, but the woman was deceived and became a transgressor.*
> 1 Timothy 2:14

Elsewhere, in the context of exhorting the Church to be on her guard against the message of false teachers, he says:

> *I am afraid that as the serpent deceived Eve by his cunning, your thoughts will be led astray from a sincere and pure devotion to Christ.*
>
> 2 Corinthians 11:3

These two references to the specific deception of Eve not only show that Paul agreed with the specific details found in the account of the Fall, i.e. that the serpent deceived Eve first, but also that he thought the entire Genesis narrative concerning Adam and Eve was true and authoritative for the Church in Corinth. This means that the Apostle Paul would expect us to have the same attitude today.

> *"...Paul agreed with the specific details found in the account of the Fall... he thought the entire Genesis narrative concerning Adam and Eve was true and authoritative..."*

The last Adam

The apostle Paul has already argued in Romans 5 that justification is necessary because of the Fall of Adam and the subsequent entrance of sin into the world. In another letter to the Corinthian church Paul brings a sustained theological argument for the physical resurrection of the dead, an integral part of the Gospel. In his argument Paul draws parallels and contrasts between Jesus Christ and the first man Adam. His frequent references to the Creation and Fall narratives in Genesis can only be applicable to his argument if they do, in fact, depict true historical events.

Paul lays out his argument that Christ is the first fruits of the resurrection in 1 Corinthians 15:20: "But in fact Christ has been raised from the dead, the first fruits of those who have fallen asleep". He then proceeds to make a parallel and a contrast with Adam: "For as by a man came death, by a man has come also the resurrection of the dead. For as in Adam all die, so also in Christ shall all be made alive" (1 Corinthians 15:21-22). Paul highlights that both men stand in some way as representative heads of humanity and each has affected human history in contrasting ways. It was both "a man" that brought death, and "a man" that defeated death. The emphasis is on the humanity of Christ as the model for the future resurrection from the dead. Paul states that through the man Christ Jesus, the death brought by Adam will be ultimately defeated (1 Corinthians 15:26).

Later in the same chapter, Paul is speaking specifically about the resurrection body and the natural body. He again chooses to use the contrast between Adam and Jesus. He writes, "The first man Adam became a living being; the last Adam became a life-giving spirit" (1 Corinthians 15:45). Here, he explicitly confirms the Genesis account that Adam was the first ever human.

> "...through the man Christ Jesus, the death brought by Adam will be ultimately defeated."

He continues, "The first man was from the earth, a man of dust; the second man is from heaven" (1 Corinthians 15:47), confirming the Genesis account

> "...the good news is that there is another who has come: The Last Adam..."

that Adam was formed from the dust of the ground. And finally, he argues, "Just as we have borne the image of the earthy, we will also bear the image of the heavenly" (1 Corinthians 15:49). Our ultimate destiny is not to bear the image of the first Adam, but to bear the image of the last Adam.

The first Adam was created innocent and perfect. He was given responsibility over humanity. It was through his one act of disobedience that sin and death entered the word (Romans 5:12). This sin spread to all the descendants of Adam, severing their relationship with God and placing mankind in the likeness of Adam – guilty of sin and deserving of death (Romans 6:23). It is just as God warned back in the Garden (Genesis 2:17). Yet the good news is that there is another who has come: The Last Adam – who is perfect, innocent and holy. He has become the new head of humanity and he came to die in our place on the cross, "tasting death for everyone" (Hebrews 2:9). It is because of His work on the cross, and the fact that He rose again, defeating death once and for all, that through him, "all will be made alive" (1 Corinthians 15:22). Those who have trusted in him by faith and "received the free gift of righteousness" (Romans 5:17) are those who "have now passed from death to life" (John 5:24; 1 John 3:14). We can now rejoice with Paul as he concludes his message about the last Adam:

> *"O death, where is your victory?*
> *O death, where is your sting?"*
> *The sting of death is sin, and the power of sin is the law; but thanks be to God, who gives us the victory through our Lord Jesus Christ.*
>
> 1 Corinthians 15: 55-57

Also available in this series...

What does the Bible really say about...

THE DAYS OF CREATION

Simon Turpin

DayOne

What does the Bible really say about... RELIGION

Simon Turpin

DayOne

Discussion questions available to download online.

dayone.co.uk

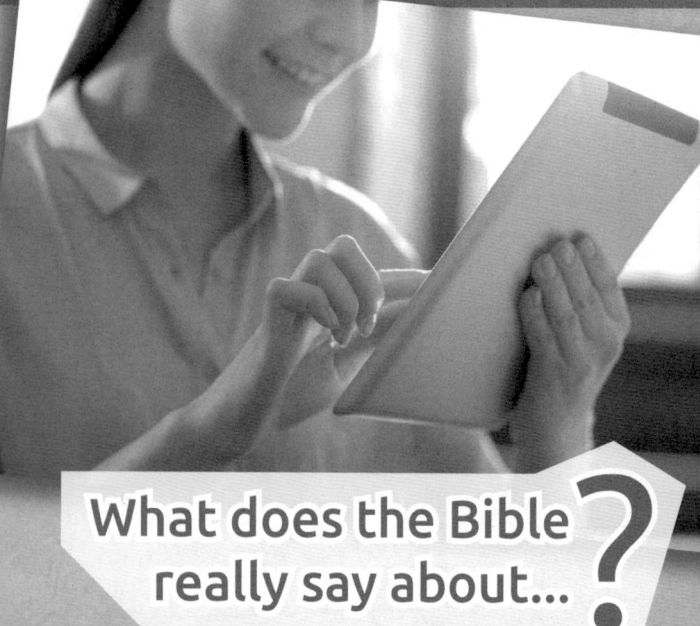

What does the Bible really say about...?